MACMILLAN
HEINEMANN
English Language Teaching

Smile please! 3

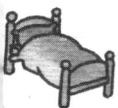
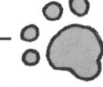

Workbook

Gabby Pritchard

Additional material by Jeanne Perrett-Tamami

Unit 1 Clothes

1. Match.

a hat

a jacket

trousers

shoes

a shirt

2. Read, look and write.

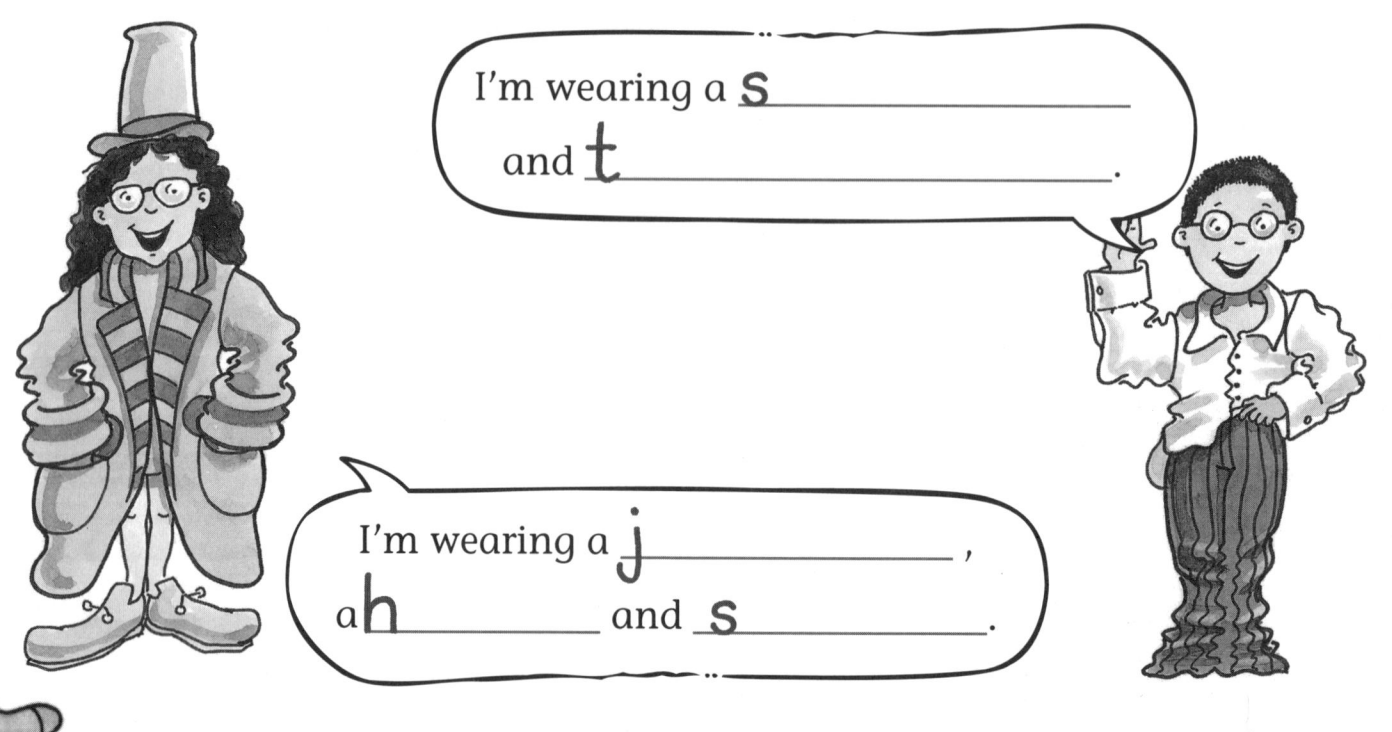

I'm wearing a s_____
and t_____.

I'm wearing a j_____,
a h_____ and s_____.

3. Read, find and colour.

blue jeans
a yellow T-shirt
an orange jumper
a pink shirt
green socks
a red jacket
a black hat
orange shorts
a pink dress
yellow shoes
a blue skirt
brown trousers

4. Sort and write.

It's a ...

socks

dress

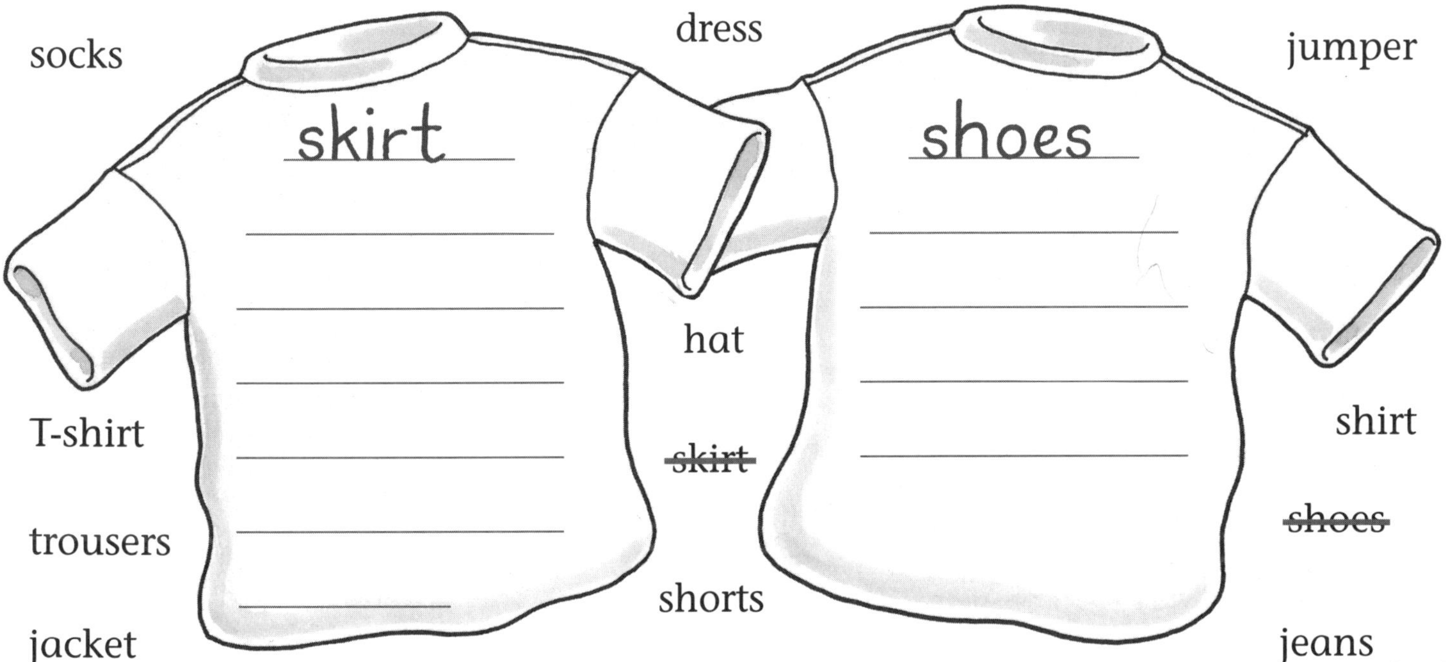

skirt
_____
_____
_____

T-shirt

trousers

jacket

hat

skirt

shorts

They're ...

jumper

shoes
_____
_____

shirt

shoes

jeans

5. Write.

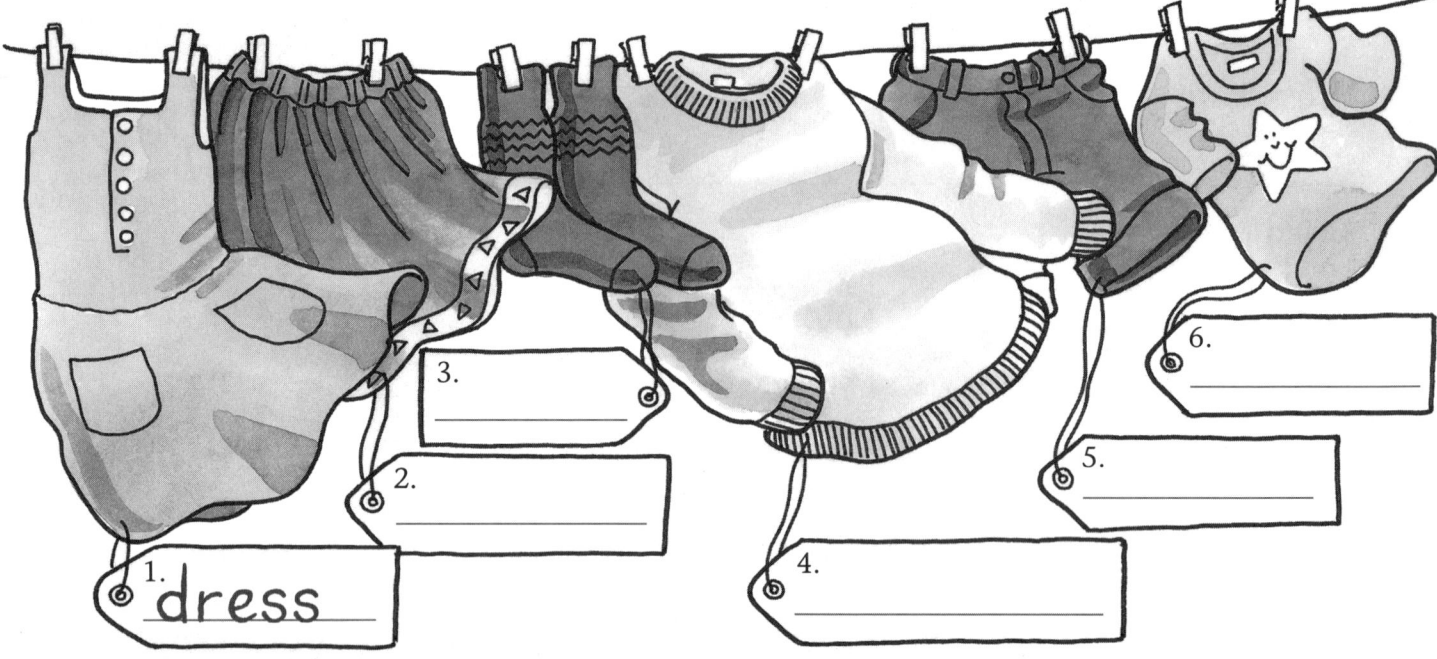

1. dress
2. _____
3. _____
4. _____
5. _____
6. _____

6. Read, find and write.

Jodie is wearing shorts. Peter is wearing a shirt.
Jack is wearing jeans. Mia is wearing a dress.

I'm Peter.

1. _____
2. _____
3. _____

7. Sort and write.

1. dress./She's/wearing/a

She's _____

2. hat/jacket./a/and/He's/wearing/a

_____

3. He's/trousers./wearing/and/jumper/a

_____

8. Look and write.

1. She's wearing a T-shirt, _____

and _____

2. She's _____

_____

3. _____

_____

9. Look and write.

In my suitcase there's a _jacket,_

a _____,

a pair of _____,

a pair of _____,

a pair of _____

and a _____.

10. Write a pair of or a.

1. _a pair of_ jeans

2. _____ dress

3. _____ socks

4. _____ shoes

5. _____ skirt

6. _____ trousers

7. _____ T-shirt

8. _____ coat

9. _____ trainers

10. _____ tracksuit

11. Write new/old/big/small and complete.

1. It's an

2. It's a

3. It's a

4. They're

_____ _____.

_____ _____.

_____ _____.

_____ _____.

12. Circle the correct sentence.

1. It's a skirt green.

    (It's a green skirt.)

2. They're white jeans.

    They're jeans white.

3. It's an orange jacket.

    It's a jacket orange.

4. They're shoes grey.

    They're grey shoes.

13. Colour and write.

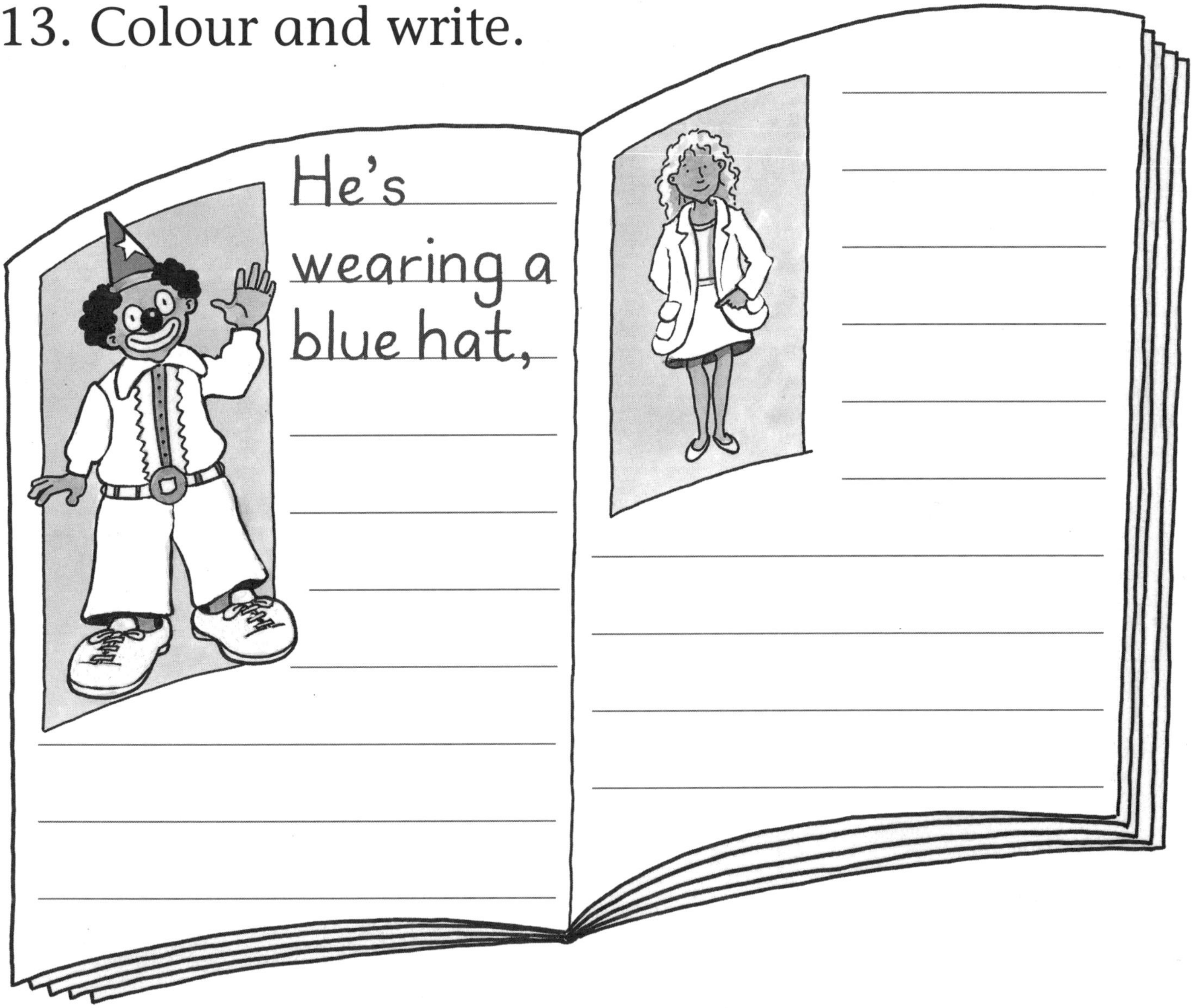

He's
wearing a
blue hat,
_____
_____
_____

_____
_____
_____
_____
_____
_____

14. Draw and write about yourself and a friend.

I'm wearing _____

_____

_____

Now I know

- [ ] I'm wearing...
- [ ] He's/She's wearing...
- [ ] It's a shirt./They're socks.
- [ ] Clothes
- [ ] Old/new
- [ ] Colours

Unit 2   I'm hungry.

1. Find and write the number.

hungry 3   bored ☐   thirsty ☐   hot ☐   tired ☐

2. Write True or False.

I'm bored.

I'm hot.

I'm tired.

I'm thirsty.

1. _____   2. _____   3. _____   4. _____

3. Match and write.

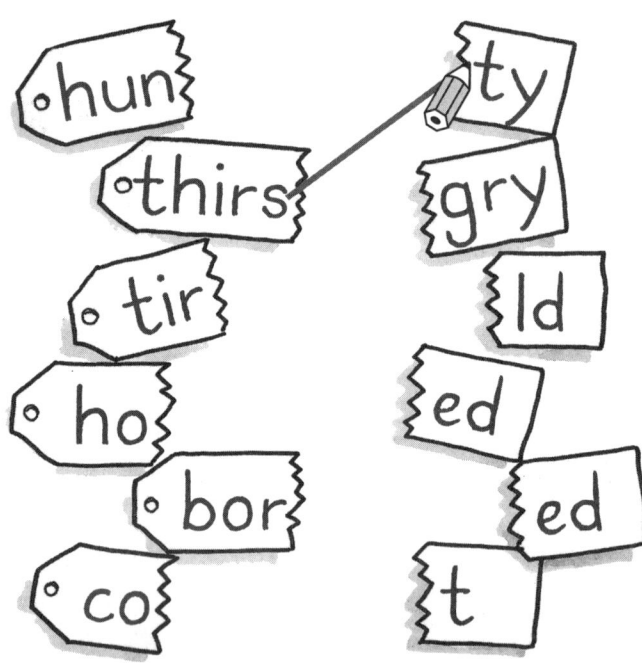

hun · · ty
thirs · gry
tir · ld
ho · ed
bor · ed
co t

1. <u>thirsty</u> _____
2. _____
3. _____
4. _____
5. _____
6. _____

4. Write.

I'm _____

_____

_____

_____

_____

_____

5. Sort and write.

chadswin   teckaj    krind   cie macre

1. _____ 2. _____ 3. _____ 4. _____

6. Find and write the number.

I want to go to bed.   4

I want to go home.   ☐

I want a drink.   ☐

I want a sandwich.   ☐

7. Look and write.

1. I'm _____.

I <u>want</u> a

s_____.

2. I'm _____.

I _____ an

i_____.

3. I'm _____.

I _____ a

j_____.

8. Read, look and write.

| bored | ice cream | thirsty | bored | home | tired | want |

Mum, I'm **bored.**

I want to go _____.

1

2

I'm hot. I _____

an _____.

No.

No.

Now I'm _____.

3

4

And I'm t_____.

Mum …

I'm b_____.

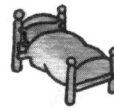

9. Look and write.

1

2

3

4

5

6

1. It's hungry.

2. It's not.

3. He's _____.

4. She's _____.

5. I'm _____.

6. You're _____.

10. Write.

I'm = I am

You're = _____

He's = _____

She's = _____

I'm not = I am not

You're not = _____

He's not = _____

She's not = _____

11. Look and write.

1. <u>bread</u>

2. _____

3. _____

4. _____

5. _____

6. _____

12. Circle the correct sentence.

1. (She's sad.)

   She's not sad.

2. He's not thirsty.

   He's thirsty.

3. They're happy.

   They're not happy.

13. Look and write.

1. <u>He's bored</u>.

2. _____.

3. _____.

14. Write.

1

I'm _____

2
_____

Now write words and letters in the square.

h	u	n	g	r	y	r	s

3

_____

4

_____

Can your friend find the words?

5
_____

6
_____

Now I know

- [ ] I'm hungry/bored/tired/thirsty/ cold/hot/happy/sad. I'm not … .
- [ ] I want a/an … . I want to … .
- [ ] I/you/he/she/it … .
- [ ] Food/drink

Unit 2

What time is it?

1. Find and write.

1. It's a quarter to five. | C |

2. It's a quarter past two. | |

3. It's six o'clock. | |

4. It's half past eleven. | |

a

b

c

d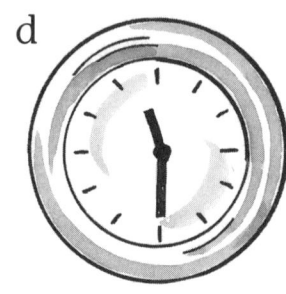

2. Read and draw.

It's a quarter past eight.

It's half past ten.

It's a quarter to seven.

3. Sort and write.

1

time/is/What/it?

W _____

_____

2

o'clock./It's/eight

_____

_____

3

a/It's/quarter/three./to

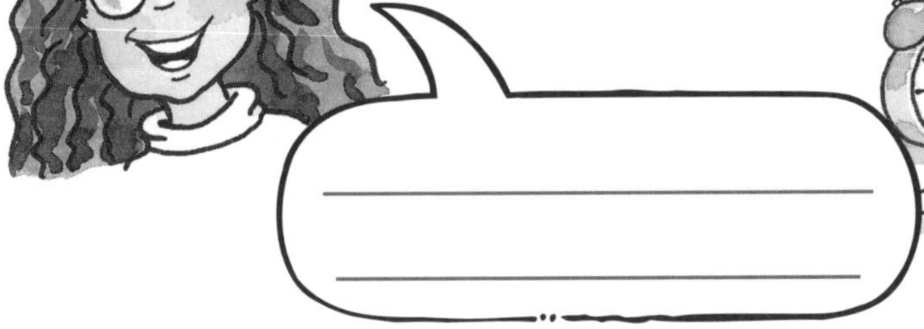

_____

_____

4

past/quarter/a/nine./It's

_____

_____

4. Look and write.

a

b
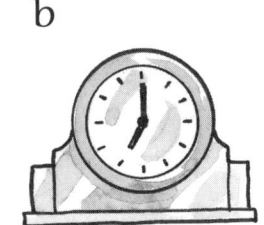

c
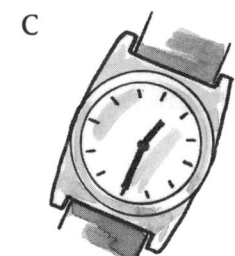

d
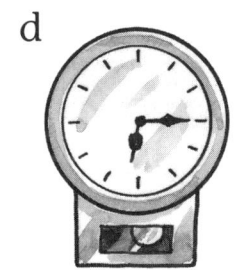

What time is it?

a. It's a quarter to eleven.

b. It's _____

c. _____

d. _____

5. Read and write.

| She's | What's | He's | homework. | ~~doing?~~ |

1
What's Dan **doing?**

2
_____ doing _____

3
_____ Jill doing?

4
_____ playing with friends.

6. Look and write.

| having dinner | ~~getting up~~ | having a shower | going to sleep |

1 She's getting up.

2 He's _____

3 She's _____

4 He's _____

7. Look and answer.

1

What time is it?
It's a quarter past seven.
What's Anna doing?
She's _____

2

What time is it?

_____

What's Anna doing?

_____

3

What time is it?

_____

What's Anna doing?

_____

4

What time is it?

_____

What's Anna doing?

_____

8. Circle and write what you have for breakfast.

I have _____

_____

_____ for breakfast.

9. Read and complete the chart.

| On Mondays I have cereal, orange juice and a banana. |
| On Tuesdays I have a sandwich, salad and an apple. |
| On Wednesdays I have salad, a hamburger, spaghetti and a banana. |

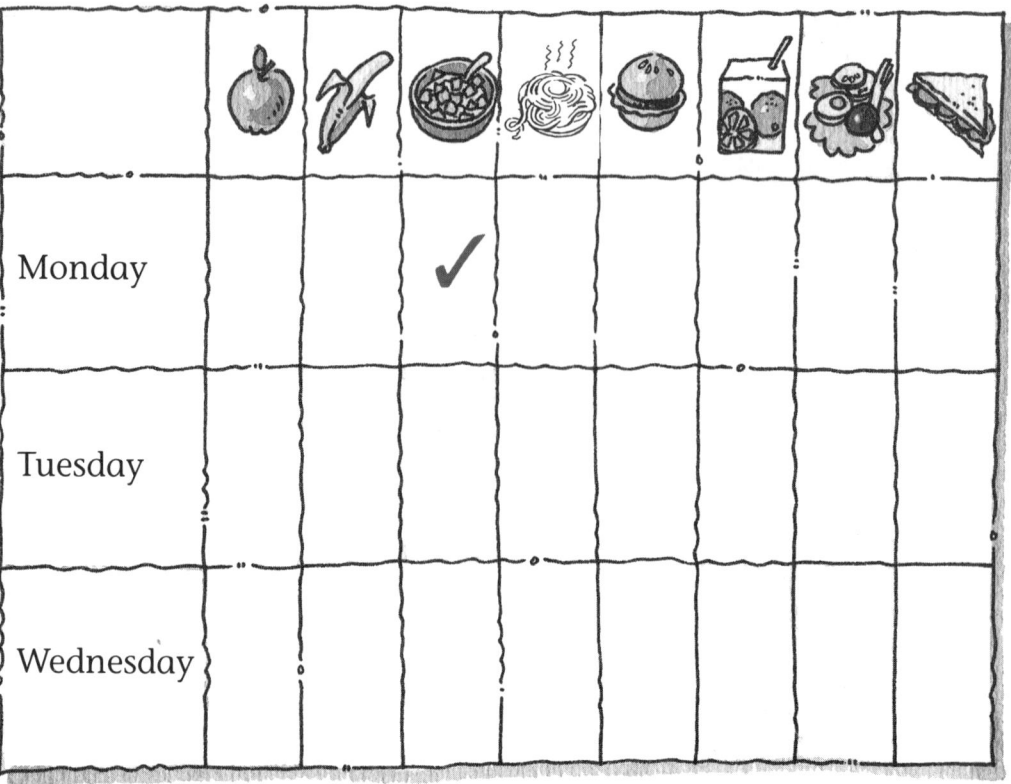

10. Look and complete.

1. Suzy _____ up at half past seven.

2. Then she _____ a shower.

3. She _____ dressed.

4. She _____ breakfast.

5. Then she _____ to school.

6. She _____ her homework.

7. She _____ with her friends.

8. At half past nine, she _____ to sleep.

Unit 3

11. Ask your friends and write.

What do you have for ... ?

	Friend 1	Friend 2
Breakfast		
Dinner		

Now I know

- [ ] What time is it? It's ... .
- [ ] What's he/she doing?
- [ ] He's/She's eating dinner.
- [ ] He/She ... at half past seven.
- [ ] I have ... for breakfast/dinner.

Unit 4 When's your birthday?

1. Write.

W_____ your b_____?

My birthday is in _____.

2. Find and circle.

| January |
| February |
| March |
| April |
| May |
| June |
| July |
| August |
| September |
| October |
| November |
| December |

S	U	J	U	N	E	R	D	O
E	S	A	P	R	I	L	E	C
P	M	N	O	A	N	O	C	T
T	A	U	G	U	S	T	E	O
E	Y	A	J	U	L	Y	M	B
M	A	R	C	H	K	R	B	E
B	S	Y	L	T	S	M	E	R
E	F	E	B	R	U	A	R	Y
R	N	O	V	E	M	B	E	R

3. Write the months.
Then write your special days.

January	F _ _ _ _ _ _ _ _ _	M _ _ _ _ _
A _ _ _ _ _	M _ _	J _ _ _
J _ _ _	A _ _ _ _ _ _	S _ _ _ _ _ _ _ _ _
O _ _ _ _ _ _ _	N _ _ _ _ _ _ _ _	D _ _ _ _ _ _ _ _ Christmas

4. Look and complete for your special days.

Christmas _____ is in December. _____

My birthday _____ is in _____

_____ is in _____

_____ is in _____

5. Find and write.

5th   13th

8th

17th

21st

23rd

14th

31st

29th

27th

20th

10th

6th

16th

24th

25th

18th   12th   30th   7th

May

SUN	MON	TUE	WED	THU	FRI	SAT
1st	2nd	3rd	4th	5th		
	9th		11th			
15th				19th		
22nd				26th		28th

6. Read and match.

first

fourteenth

third

eighth

twenty-second

tenth

thirtieth

twenty-ninth

7. Write.

What's the date today?

It's _____

8. Sort and write.

birthday?/When's/your	on/is/birthday/twenty-fifth/My/March./of/the

W _____ ?
_____

_____
_____

9. Ask your friends and write their birthdays.

Date	Month	Name	Date	Month	Name
	January			July	
	February			August	
25th	March	Freddy		September	
	April			October	
	May			November	
	June			December	

10. Write.

a. thirty _30_

b. forty _____

c. fifty _____

d. sixty _____

e. seventy _____

f. eighty _____

g. ninety _____

h. one hundred _____

11. Match.

We write:

a. 2nd June

b. 15th May

c. 21st December

d. 12th June

e. 8th May

f. 3rd December

We say:

the fifteenth of May

the twenty-first of December

the second of June

the eighth of May

the twelfth of June

the third of December

When's your birthday?

My birthday is on the _____ of _____.

Unit 4

12. Look and complete.

It's my birthday. I've got lots of _____ and a big

_____. There are nine _____ on the

_____. My birthday is on _____.

13. Read and complete.

January is the $first$ month.

M_____ is the third month.

October is the _____.

S_____ is the ninth _____.

F_____ second _____.

July _____.

14. Write the months in the correct order.

F_____

  N_____

    D_____

A_____

  M_____

  J_____

 J_____

    O_____

A_____

 J_____

  M_____

S_____

1. January _____

2. _____

3. _____

4. _____

5. _____

6. _____

7. _____

8. _____

9. _____

10. _____

11. _____

12. _____

Now I know

☐ When's … ?

☐ It's in … .

☐ What's the date today? It's … .

☐ When's your birthday?

☐ It's on the 1st of July.

☐ Months of the year

Unit 5   My House

1. Find and write the number.

1. bedroom   2. living room   3. kitchen   4. bathroom

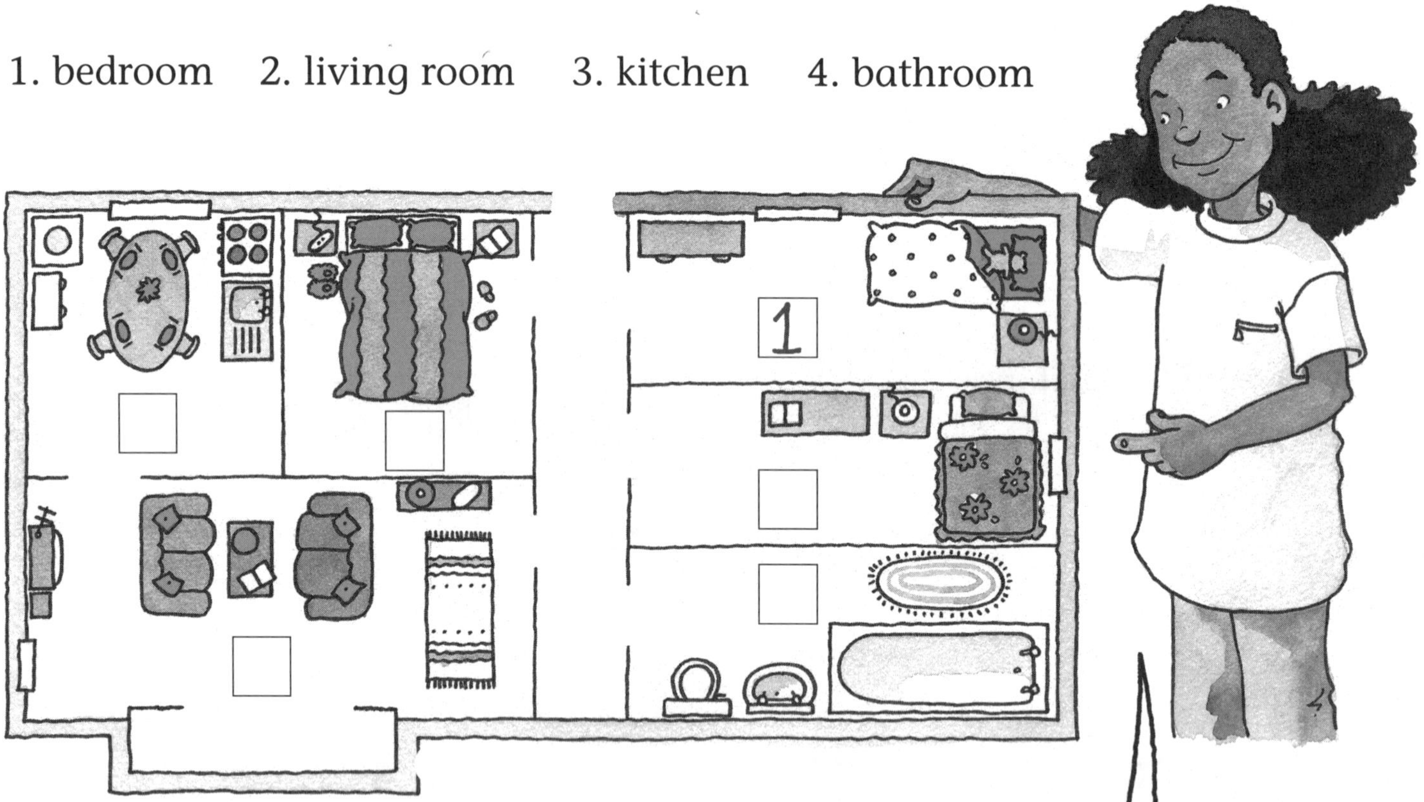

2. Look, read and complete.

I live in a house. There's a k_____

and a l_____ r_____.

There are three b_____ and

a b_____.

3. Read and write the name.

Sam:	I live in a flat. There's a living room, a small kitchen and a bathroom. There are three bedrooms.
Anna:	I live in a house. There are three bedrooms and two bathrooms. There's a living room and a kitchen.
Ken:	I live in a flat. There are two bedrooms. There's a living room, a kitchen, and a small bathroom.

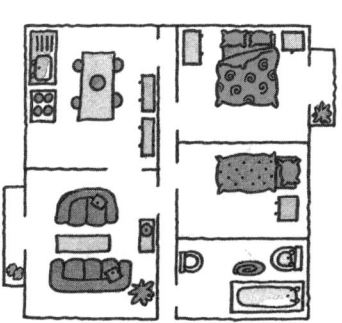 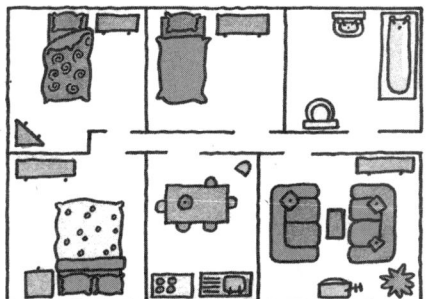 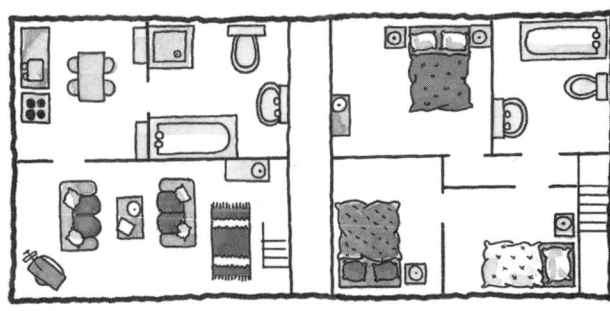

1. _____ 2. _____ 3. _____

4. Read and write. Then complete the picture.

1. <u>bedroom</u>

> There's a kitchen and a living room. There's a small bathroom. There are three bedrooms.

2. _____

3. _____

_____

4. _____

5. _____

6. _____

5. Look and write.

Crossword (down, clue 1): t e l e v i s i o n

6. Look and write.

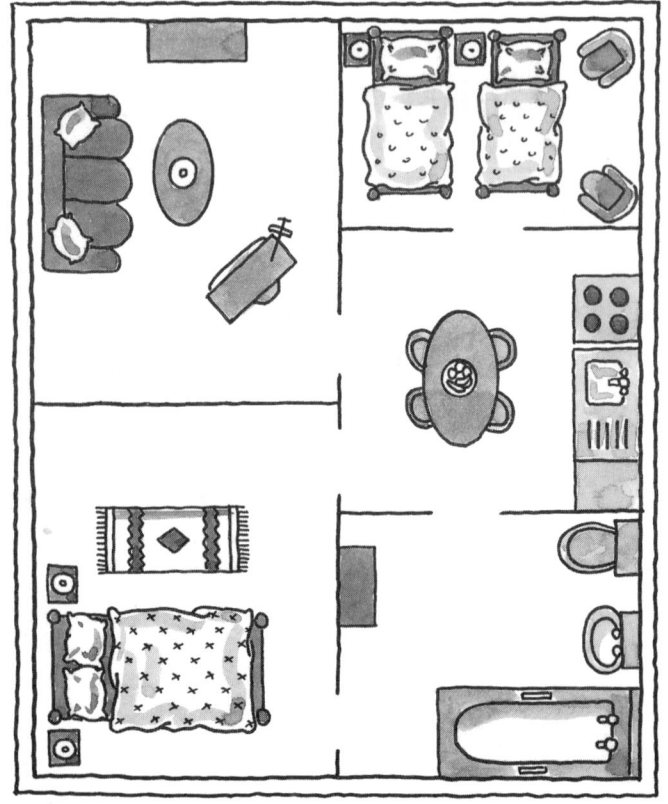

1. There's a sofa and a television in the
   _____.

2. There's a table, a sink and a cooker
   in the _____.

3. There are two beds and two chairs
   in the small _____.

4. There's a bath in the
   _____.

5. There's a bed and a rug in the big
   _____.

7. Write There's or There are.

1. _____ a bath.

2. _____ three beds.

3. _____ two sofas.

4. _____ two tables.

5. _____ a cooker.

6. _____ two sinks.

How many rooms are there?

7. _____ rooms.

8. Read and answer.

table chair cooker sink	1. Is it the bathroom? <u>No, it isn't.</u>
table chair bed rug	2. Is it the bedroom? _____
bath shower	3. Is it the kitchen? _____
rug chair sofa TV	4. Is it the living room? _____
sink table chair cooker	5. Is it the bedroom? _____

9. Match and colour.

France   Greece   Spain   UK

10. Read. Then complete.

11, West Way
Croydon
England

Dear Mike,
My name's Ben.
I live in a house in England.
Do you live in a house or a flat?
Please write to me.

Best wishes,
Ben

_____

_____

_____

Dear _____,

My name's _____

I live in a _____ in _____.

Do you _____ in a house or a

flat? Please _____ to me.

_____ wishes,

_____

11. Read and draw.

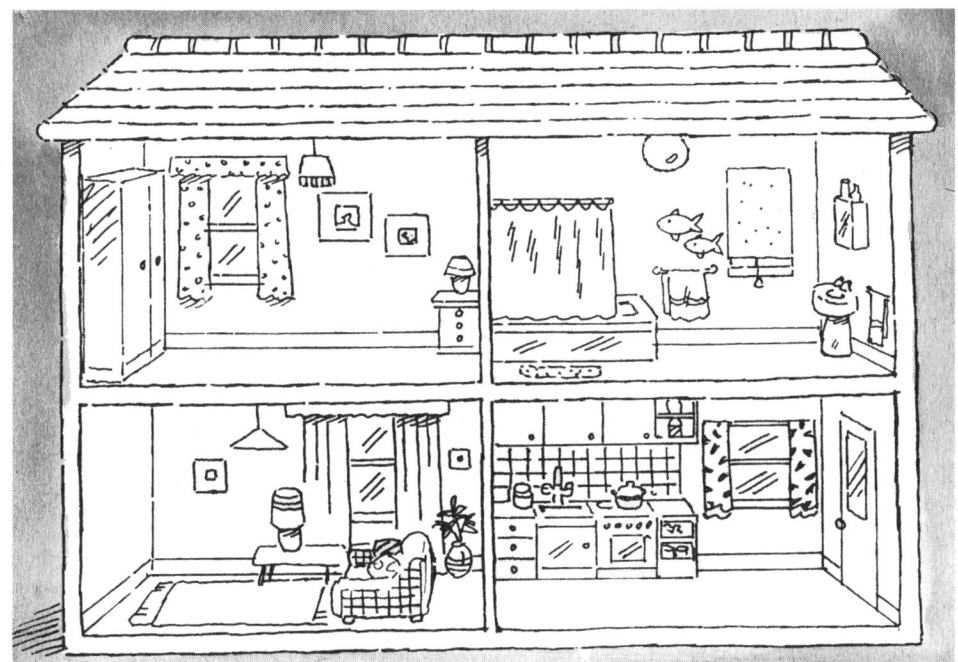

There are two beds in the bedroom.

There's a table in the kitchen.

There's a TV in the living room.

There's a chair in the bathroom.

12. Write the questions.

What's _____ ?

_____ ?

_____ ?

_____ ?

My name's Ken.

I'm 11.

I live in Japan.

I don't live in a house. I live in a flat.

13. Write about your house or flat.

There's	There are

Now I know

- [ ] I live in a house/flat.
- [ ] I don't live in a house/flat.
- [ ] There's a TV/cooker/bath.
- [ ] There are two bedrooms.
- [ ] How many ... ?
- [ ] I live in Greece.

Unit 6 The Weather

1. Find and write.

1
2
3
4
5

It's sunny. ☐3 It's raining. ☐ It's cloudy. ☐ It's snowing. ☐ It's windy. ☐

2. Sort and write.

weather/What's/like?/the

W _____
_____

It's _____.

3. Circle, write and draw.

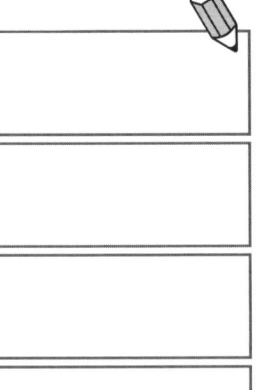

s	n	o	w	i	n	g
u	b	f	i	p	u	p
n	i	k	n	t	b	f
n	f	a	d	s	w	o
y	o	m	y	a	i	t
c	l	o	u	d	y	d
r	a	i	n	i	n	g

1. snowing _____

2. _____

3. _____

4. _____

5. _____

4. Write.

What's the weather like?

It's _____.

_____.

_____.

_____.

_____.

5. Read and answer.

Monday windy
Tuesday cloudy
Wednesday raining
Thursday sunny
Friday snowing

1. It's Thursday.
   What's the weather like?

   It's sunny.
2. It's Wednesday.
   What's the weather like?

   ____
3. It's Tuesday.
   What's the weather like?

   ____
4. It's Friday.
   What's the weather like?

   ____
5. It's Monday.
   What's the weather like?

   ____

6. Complete and answer.

What's ______________________ today?

☐ ☐ ☐ ☐

It's ______________ today.

7. Read and write.

snowing   weather   raining   sunny   hot   cold

1

What's the _____ like?

It's _____.

2

Look! Now it's _____.

3

I'm wearing a hat and a jacket. It's _____ outside.

4

Oh! Now it's _____.

And I'm _____.

Unit 6   40

8. Write the seasons.

_____   spring _____

_____   _____

9. Look and complete. Then answer.

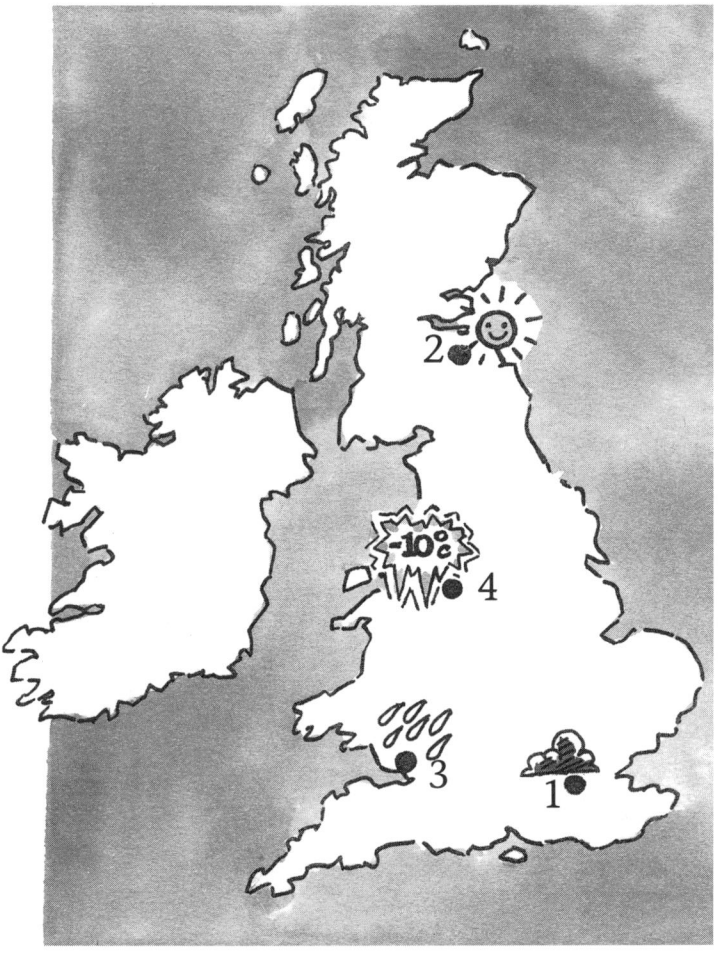

1. What's the weather like

   in London?

   It's cloudy _____.

2. _____

   _____ Edinburgh?

   _____.

3. _____

   _____ Cardiff?

   _____.

4. _____

   _____ Liverpool?

   _____.

10. Look and complete.

What are they going to do?

go to school	go to the beach
~~have breakfast~~	go to bed

1. They're going to _have breakfast_.

2. She's going to _____ _____.

3. He's going to _____ _____.

4. She's going to _____ _____.

11. Complete. Then draw for your country.

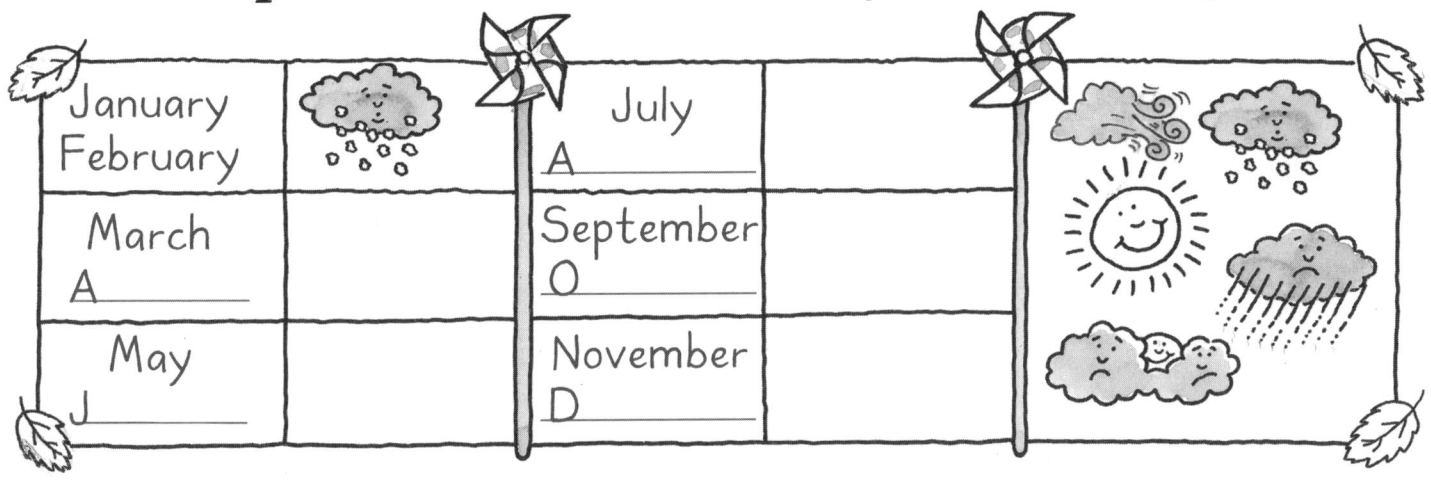

January February		July A_____	
March A_____		September O_____	
May J_____		November D_____	

12. Look at the chart. Answer the questions.

1. It's January. What's the weather like?

It's _____

2. It's July. What's the weather like?

_____

3. It's April. What's the weather like?

_____

4. It's October. What's the weather like?

_____

5. It's December. What's the weather like?

_____

Now I know

☐ What's the weather like?

☐ It's raining/snowing/windy/cloudy.

☐ It's hot/cold/wet/sunny.

☐ I'm/He's/She's going to ... .

Shopping

1. Write the prices.

book = 3 pounds	puzzle = 4 pounds	flag = 3 pounds
T-shirt = 5 pounds	kite = 7 pounds	~~ball = 6 pounds~~

£____ £6 £____

£____ £____ £____

2. Look and complete.

1. How much is the ball?

   It's ____

2. How much is the _____?

   It's £4.

3. How much is the _____?

   It's £3.

4. How much is the T-shirt?

   _____

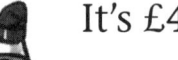

3. Read, write and add.

I want the kite, the puzzle, and the mug, please.

I want the comic book, the ball, and the puppet, please.

£7

£3

£1

£4

£2

£6

kite   £7

_____

_____

_____

Total _____

_____

_____

_____

_____

Total _____

4. Look and write the questions.

1. How much is the _____ It's £1.

2. _____ It's £2.

3. _____ It's £3.

4. _____ It's £4.

5. Read and complete the story.

| Have | any | ribbon | got | want | kite |

1

"Hello. Have you got an orange _____?"

"No, I haven't. Sorry."

2

"Excuse me. _____ you got an orange kite?"

"No, I haven't. I've _____ a green kite."

"Oh, no, I _____ an orange kite."

3

"Have you got _____ orange paper?"

"Yes, I have. Anything else?"

"Yes, I want some _____, some glue, and some string. Oh, and some wood, and some paint, please."

paint	£3
ribbon	£2
string	£1
wood	£3
glue	£2

4

5 "Look. I've got a new kite."

"It's great!"

6. Read, look and write the questions.

Have you got any wood?   Yes, I have.

How much is it?   It's £3.

_____ ribbon?   Yes, I have.

_____ It's £2.

_____ string?   Yes, I have.

_____ It's £1.

7. Look and write.

a lot of	a few
bread	biscuits

8. Look and complete.

I've got <u>a lot of</u> water.
I haven't got <u>any</u> milk.

1. I've got _____ ice cream.

2. I've got _____ sweets.

3. I haven't got _____ soup.

4. I've got _____ apples.

5. I haven't got _____ cheese.

6. I've got _____ bread.

9. Look, read and write True or False.

How much water have you got?

1

I haven't got any water. _____

How many apples have you got?

2

I've got a lot of apples. _____

How much ice cream have you got?

3

I've got a lot of ice cream. _____

How many biscuits have you got?

4

I've got a few biscuits. _True_

10. Read. Complete with a lot of/a few/any.

1. He's got _a lot of_ chocolate.

2. She hasn't got _____ sausages.

3. Has he got _____ bread?

4. I've got _____ packets of crisps. I've got three.

5. You've got _____ sweets. You've got ten packets!

6. She hasn't got _____ milk.

11. Find six toys, circle and write.

1. puppet
2. _____
3. _____
4. _____
5. _____
6. _____

Tell your friend what you want to buy.

Now I know

- [ ] How much is it/is the … ? It's … .
- [ ] Have you got a/an/any … ? I've got … .
- [ ] Yes, I have./No, I haven't.
- [ ] I want some … .
- [ ] How much/many … have you got?
- [ ] I haven't got any … .
- [ ] a lot of/a few

1. Write and colour.

Easter E ___ ___

Ea ___ ___ ___ ___ Bunny

R ___ ___ ___ ___ ___ ___

R ___ ___ ___ ___ ___

H ___ ___ ___ ___

E ___ ___ ___ ___ ___

Mother's Day

1. Read and write.

| cold | sandwich | drink | happy | tired | hungry | jacket | thirsty |

1

I'm _____.

Mum wants a _____.

2

I'm _____.

She wants a _____.

3

I'm _____.

She wants a _____.

4

Happy Mother's Day!

I'm _____!

We're _____.

2. Read, write the name and colour.

My mum is wearing a yellow shirt and jeans. She's happy!   Sam

My mum is tall. She's wearing a pink T-shirt and a blue skirt.   Maria

_____'s mum   _____'s mum

3. Now draw and write about your mum.

_____

_____

_____

_____

_____

_____

_____

_____

_____

Mother's Day

Picture Dictionary

Cut out the pictures on pages 57 and 59.
Stick them in the right place here to make
your picture dictionary.

At eight o'clock ...

he has a shower.

At half past seven ...

she gets up.

At a quarter past eight ...

she has breakfast.

At half past eight ...

he gets dressed.

At five o'clock ...

she plays with friends.

At a quarter past five ...

she does homework.

At half past six ...

he has dinner.

At nine o'clock ...

he goes to bed.

Cut out the words on page 61 and stick them in
the right place here to make your picture dictionary.

Cut out these pictures and stick them in the right place on pages 54 and 55.

Cut out these pictures and stick them in the right place on pages 54 and 55.

Cut out these words and stick them in the
right place on page 56.

sofa

television

table

sink

cooker

bed

chair

rug

bath

cupboard

kitchen

living room

bedroom

bathroom

My year

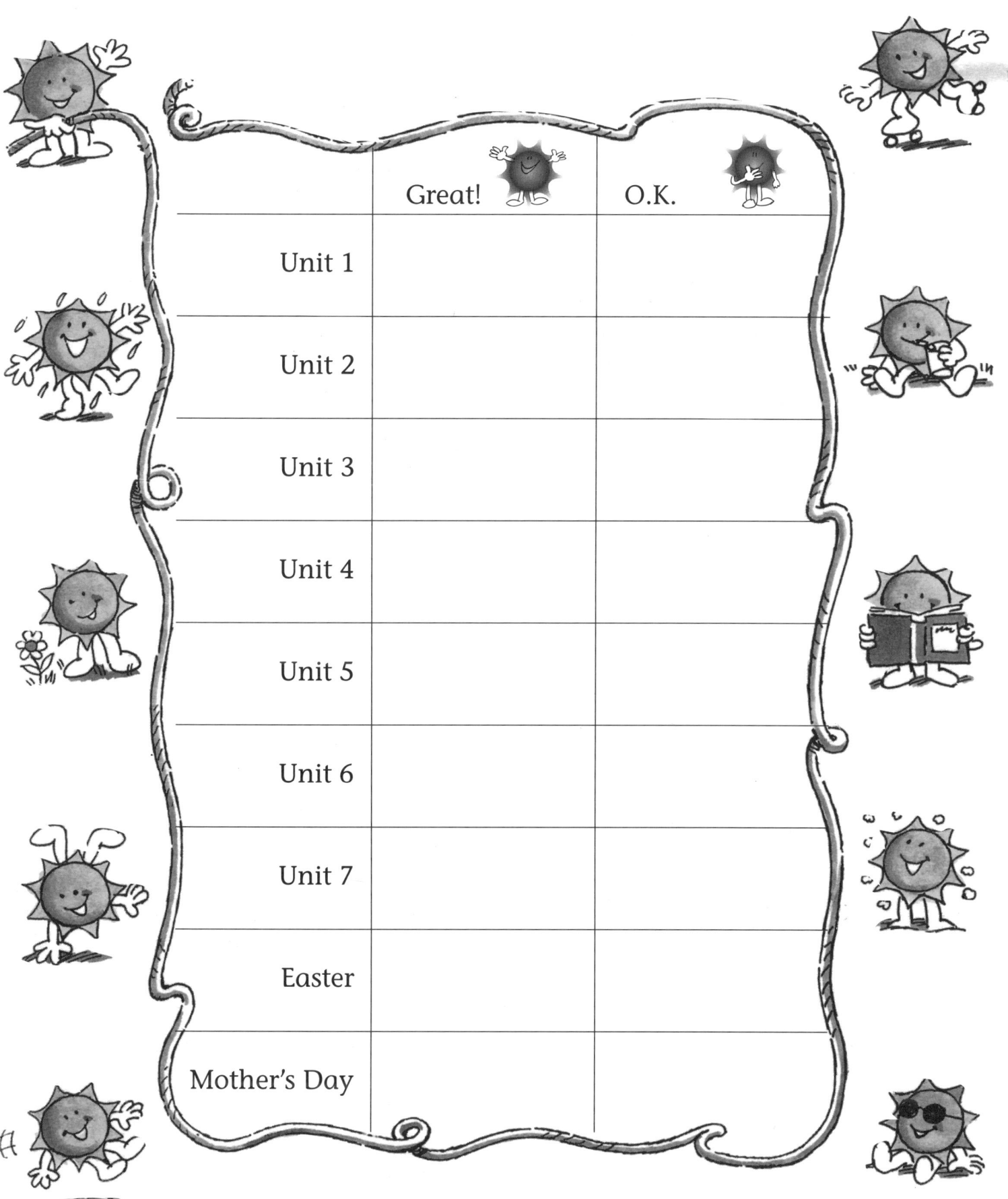

	Great!	O.K.
Unit 1		
Unit 2		
Unit 3		
Unit 4		
Unit 5		
Unit 6		
Unit 7		
Easter		
Mother's Day		

Macmillan Heinemann English Language Teaching, Oxford

A division of Macmillan Publishers Limited

Companies and representatives throughout the world

ISBN 0 435 29309 5

Based on the *Say It In English* language pack
© Dorling Kindersley Limited & World Book Inc.
Original material used by permission of Dorling Kindersley Limited.

Text, design and illustration © Macmillan Publishers Limited 1999
Heinemann is a registered trademark of Reed Educational & Professional Publishing Limited

First published 1999

Designed by The Junction.
Illustrated by Teri Gower, Michael Walsh and David Till

Cover illustrated by Teri Gower and designed by Sue Vaudin

Printed and bound in Great Britain by Redwood Books, Trowbridge, Wiltshire

99 00 01 02 03 10 9 8 7 6 5 4 3 2 1